Shentama

Second Edition
Copyright © 2024 Phil Moore
On behalf of the Prophet Tobias
All Rights Reserved

The moral rights of the Author have been asserted
Design: Phil Moore
Published by Virtual Worlds
virtualworlds.com.au

Hardback Edition
ISBN: 978-0-6459806-5-3

PREFACE

These words are to be read by the heart
Not by the mind
By the spirit
Not by the self
With imagination
Not literal intent

For the words are merely metaphors
Of something that is beyond language
They are the beginning
Not the end
Their meanings are many
As many as who read them
And they are constantly changing
As you, the reader, change.

Find in these words your own meaning
Let them speak in your own voice
As you become the teacher, and I
Merely the wordsmith

The four tenets of understanding

- ∞ Death is not an end, it is a renewal of life.
- ∞ Choice, not chance, determines your destiny.
- ∞ Freedom means allowing others to also be free.
- ∞ Everything begins and ends with you.

I am not the way
I am a light unto myself only
Let no man seek to make ritual of what I say
Nor legend of what I do

My light is but a glimmer
A pale indication of incommunicable knowledge
The brighter light is within you
And that will show your way
Which is different from my own
Yet the same

I hope these words help set you on the path
But it is your path
If they awake in you a spectre of your self
Lead on
I can do no more

There is more to be learned from nature
Than can ever be expressed in words
Than can ever be read in books
Than can ever be told by Masters

Let the glory of life be your teacher
The humble ant has a greater understanding of its
    place and purpose
Than many a scholar

The master who expects you to follow in his steps
Is no Master
The teacher who allows you to learn only one thing
  and not another
Is no Teacher
The leader who demands obedience
  and would control your thoughts
Is no Leader

One who seeks to divert you from your path
Is insecure in their own
And not worthy of esteem

But those who are secure in their path
Desire not to lead others from theirs
And do not want esteem

The wise teacher acts as though fanning a flame
At first slowly and gently
A little at a time

As the flame grows in knowledge
It is strengthened by wisdom
And the teacher can fan more fervently
When the flame no longer needs fanning
The teacher must find another student

For wisdom cannot be given
Cannot be communicated
Cannot be bestowed
It can only be revealed

The truly wise man is silent
He has no desire to speak, but should one ask
He teaches not for himself
But for those who would listen
  and seek understanding
Ask and he will answer
But do not wait for him to speak first
For nothing is more eloquent
Than that which is said in silence

Of yourself
The only person whose opinion matters is your own
If you believe you are weak
Then you will have no strength
If you believe you are ugly
Then beauty will go unseen
If you believe you are poor
Then you will never know abundance
If you believe you are unloved
Then you shall live out your days in loneliness

It is in your eyes only the judgment is made
The opinion of others has no meaning for you
Unless you give it meaning

The world that you know and the life that you live
Are not the cause of your sorrows
But the result

Believe only in that which makes you happy
And you will be happy
Believe you have strength and you will have it
Believe you are beautiful and you will be it
Believe you are wealthy and you will become it
Believe you are loved and you will never be alone

Believe
And it will come to pass
Your life can be made joyous or tragic
According to your expectations

We each create our own reality
Build our own fences
Construct our own walls
To scale the walls you must first recognize
  that they are there
Then look beyond

The self is not limited
It knows no boundaries
Recognizes no division
Those that you perceive are caused by belief
The fences are plumbed by you alone

Life is defined by possibility
Not by limitation
See past the horizon of what is
To the greater vision of what could be
The extent of your limitations is a measure
Of the space between ignorance and understanding

Let judgment be your tool
Not your master
It is the furniture of the mind
Giving order to chaos
Understanding to confusion
But if it become an obstacle
Remove it
Change it
Discard it altogether

Do not make of your home a prison
Do not let one order rule your mind
One understanding refuse all others
This is the difference
  between knowledge and wisdom

What exists physically
  exists first in thought and feeling
With this wisdom alone
  you can change your life at will
Control your own destiny

Experience follows expectation
What you perceive as possible becomes so
What you do not, does not
What you believe about yourself defines who you are
And what your experience of reality will be

Whatever you are capable of imagining
You are capable of achieving
The only limitations upon one self
Are those one chooses to accept
There is nothing that cannot be realized
There is nothing that cannot be changed

The drama of reality is first written
In the pages of the mind
Thought becomes desire
Desire becomes action
Action becomes experience
The writer becomes the actor
And the drama that is called life
Is guided by the All-In-All

And it has but one purpose
To know self
Every moment you are changed by your experience
You grow closer to understanding
As your thoughts and deeds define who you are

You are creator and created both
And so is everybody else…

Seek always to learn from life
Whatever trials
Whatever joys
Eke out the lesson from it
Enrichment can be gained from every encounter
From every experience

There is never a moment when you are not learning
There is never a thought
  that does not become a part of you
Or deed that does not reflect your understanding
The fact you live shows you have learned so much
And have so much yet to learn
Every moment of your life fulfills this purpose

For the purpose of all education
Of all learning
Is to know nothing

That is everything

As you are a part of the All-In-All
So the All-In-All is a part of you
You are the eternal spark of life
Made manifest

Yet you are unique
As a window of clear glass
Allow the light to shine through you
Without resistance

Without judgment
Be clear in your be-ing
And be seen by all
Who look to the window for light

To be in light is to be as a beast in the wilderness
To bend like a tree in the wind
To flow like the restless waters
It is to be one with the All-In-All
Acting in accord
Without judgment
Needing no other to fill the spaces
For there are none

To eat when there is food
Work when there is purpose
Play when there is pleasure
And sleep when there is need

To be simple in desires and careless of possessions
To be in accord with the earth
  and all that dwell upon it
To be aware of the energy in
  everything around you
That is the All-In-All

To know for a certainty that nothing in all of creation
Is without purpose
Without reason
And to respect that purpose
Even though it is unknown to you

For there is no backward path
All paths lead ever forward
By thought given form through word and action
Moment by moment
Life by life

Find the truth of this
And all misfortune is overcome
There is value in every circumstance
Meaning in every deed

In every thought
Every impulse
Every movement of the spirit
You are creating
And with each creation a little of yourself
Is given unto it
How else could you know the All-In-All
If you were not a part of it?
How else could you know your Self
If the All-In-All were not a part of you?

Every facet of creation
From word to rock
From song to bended knee
From a star to a blade of grass
From a city to a drop of rain
All of it is complete within and as part
Of the All-In-All

Creation is boundless
Though you give of yourself to every moment
You are never depleted
Infinite
Unending
Inexhaustible
You are creation
And creator combined

Creativity is thought
Everything you do is first begun in thought
An action of the spirit
Expressed in thought
Given form by deed and purpose

The world you know is a reflection of your truth
It changes as you change
You create it
You control it
You are responsible for it

Your creation is never lost
Even unto the past
Though the moment passes
Though the mind forgets
Your creation is now and always
A part of the All-In-All
Which is your Self

Nothing is ever destroyed
Merely transformed
There is only action and stillness
Through action is change effected
Through stillness is change prepared

For time is an illusion
There is no distinction of Past and Future
Only Now
The Forever-Now

And time is capricious
Ever moving in all directions
An ocean of remembrances
With tides and flows
Waves and ripples
The only place you will find certainty
Is in the Forever-Now
In the experience of the Present
What was true for you in another time
Is no longer true for you Now

Therefore
Think not on the Past
Nor concern yourself with the Future
But know that both are created in the Present
The point where spirit and flesh meet
The point of Creation
The timeless moment
The singularity of Self

You form your reality now
All of your reality
And as you change so reality changes with you
You can change anything in your life you desire
There is nothing within the bounds
Of earthly experience that cannot be made manifest

Your world and everything in it
Is created by you
And as such
Can be changed by you
Believe in your own power
Believe you can become
And you will
This you already do a thousand times a day

The gift of prophecy is the ability to read time
To see the Now in all its manifestations
To know that anything is possible
And everything is fixed
Fate and free will are two sides of the same coin

Therefore true prophecy is fluid
It is changed by your choices
And by the choices of others
Which are also your own
Which are known and unknown
Infinite and resolute

No beginning or end
Without measure
Without limit
The infinite vista of the Forever-Now
Laid bare and inscrutable

We are all divine fragments of creation
And we are all artists
Painting our lives upon the universe
Enacting the drama we have ourselves set down

As an actor immersed in your part
This drama is the only world you know
Because you make it so
If you but looked beyond the stage you would see
An even greater world
One cannot know the spirit but by its actions
In expression of self is the self made known
In action is it revealed

One cannot look upon its face
Or speak its name
It is invisible and unknown
But the expression is seen
And by this can the cause be known

For as you think
So you are
As the mind moves
So the body becomes
It can be found in the lines of the hand
In the texture of the eye
In the shape of the face
And the form of the torso
In the color of the hair
And the size of the foot
In the curve of the ear
And the structure of the cell
It is visible and invisible
In every part of your body

Your inner self made manifest
A spiritual creation
A work of art
Sculpted by the All-In-All

It is the divine vehicle of expression
You personal temple
There is nothing of your Self
  that is not expressed in it

As your body is an expression of Self
So Self is an expression of spirit
Which is an expression of the All-In-All
Which is an expression of spirit
Which is an expression of Self
Which is your body

And as body, mind and spirit are indivisible
So too are the myriad forms of the All-In-All

You are not your body
You are more than molded clay
You are a tree
A mountain
A drop of rain
A breath of air
A thunderbolt
A song

The All-In-All
The universal nature
The perfect oneness of all that is
The All within you
The you within All

Yet you are unique unto the world
There is no-one quite like you
In all the eons of existence
From before the beginning
To beyond the end

There is not a one to compare you

You are
For all that you are
Special and beloved
The world could not exist without you
And the universe could not be were it not for you

Do not forget this

Know that you are worthy
Know that you are strong
Know that you are gifted
Know that you are unique

Know that you have power
Know that you have support
Know that you are eternal
Know that you are loved

Let no one take from you these words
And take them not from another
For they too are beloved
Think of yourself as beautiful
For you are
Think of your body as beautiful
For it is
Think of your thoughts, feelings and desires
As wondrous and unique

And think of the world in which you live
As the magical reflection that it is
To love yourself then is easy

Equally
Any imperfection in your world
Is your own self made manifest
When you feel inadequate
When you feel powerless
It is your own self you confront
A challenge you have set yourself
From which to learn and grow

Accept the challenge
Face your demons
Defer the lesson no longer
New adventures await you
Beyond the dread mountain

For life is a quest
To fulfill the legend that is you
To seek and discover your self
And realize the power within

So deny yourself nothing in the name of virtue
Accept what is in your nature
Lest you starve your self of joy
And the true lesson goes unlearned

The only opinion that matters is your own
In your eyes only is the judgment made
The verdict of others has no store
If you refuse it

Life is an inherently selfish act
It is to be conscious of self
To have respect for self
To have love for self
To do nothing which would harm self
Which would impede self
Which would burden self

You do not abuse or harm another
For to do so reflects upon self
You would not deny another
For such an act denies one self
And you would not enslave another
Though you gain dominion over all the world
For it is only your self you enslave

To be selfish, therefore, is to be selfless
To give freely of oneself
With no expectation of reward or acclaim
With no onus of obligation
In serving others one is serving self
Whereas to be self-serving serves no-one

So feel not guilty for selfish actions
Guilt is a barricade to life
It denies you knowledge
Denies you choice
It is to be afraid of oneself
Ashamed of your reflection
Recognize the cause comes from within
Then you can understand and overcome it

And do not fear your emotions
They are neither good nor bad
They just are

To deny what you feel is to deny yourself expression
You are not separate from your emotions
Do not ignore or hide from them
Whatever the feeling
Be it good or bad as you see it
Let it be expressed
Let it flow from your being
Release it
Channel it
Use it

Every feeling unexpressed lies in wait
Like a puma coiled to pounce
Ever growing in strength
Until the barricade fails
And you can deny them no longer

And yet
To be free of emotion
To travel the path yielding and supple
Without judgment or enmity
Is to abide in the All-In-All

Not to deny your feelings
Not to control or suppress them
But to not be ruled by them either
They are, after all, nothing more or less
Than a contradiction of self
Recognize this
Revel in it
And you separate emotion from action
Passion from deed
And thought from desire

For we are known by our actions
We are judged by our actions
And we adjudge others the same

The truly strong do not boast their strength
The truly wise do not brandish their wisdom
The truly wealthy do not flaunt their prosperity
The truly powerful do not assert their dominion

To lie in truth
Is to not contend with life
To eschew the judgment of others
To have nothing to prove
And therefore nothing to fear

We each have own point-of-view
None is any more right or wrong than another
Each is equally valid and equally invalid

For the nature of Truth is irrepressible
It knows no limits and has no name
Even to call it Truth implies an antithesis

It is simplicity
Easily recognized
But never understood
All encumbrances have a truth
And with it, an untruth
Their limitations hide the greater Truth
Which is unknowable

All things abide in Truth
There is no thing that is not true
That which we call a lie abides in Truth
It is judgmental expression
Creative thought
Directed by will into whatever form one chooses
It is not false therefore
How can it be?

It is the All-In-All as expressed by you
In every thought
Every action
You abide in Truth
A Truth that is beyond words
Beyond deception

It is the only truth worth knowing
It is that which is found within
No-one, no matter how learned
Can tell you that truth by which to live your life
And if they be truly wise
They would not presume to do so

My truth is for me alone and will never serve another
If these words help to light your way that is good
But let them be the guide to your own path
And not the path you follow

While these words are but a guide
They hope to give greater understanding
To teach and enlighten
But if you learn nothing else from these words
Learn this at least:

All those actions and events
All those catalysts of knowledge
For which you have no time
You have encountered for a reason
What that reason is only you can discover

It is by the reflection that the face is known
Through understanding of the outward expression
The inner becomes clear
Through interaction with all
  that is apart from your self
You find the stillness of within

Look around
And you will see your self
  reflected in the smallest of things
All knowledge is good
Even that not yet understood
Every grain of learning is valuable and can be used
Each lesson adding to the wealth of your experience
Once learned it cannot be unlearned
It is owned by you
Becomes a part of you
And need never be learned again

For there is only one lesson
Only one purpose to life
Which is: to learn to love
And there is only one way to do this
Which is to experience it
To be in accord with the All-In-All
To live

As with all things Love is unique to us all
But I offer these reflections:

Love is not a weapon
Love is not a burden
Love is not an excuse

Love does not emancipate
Love does not enlighten
Love does not nourish

Love is not proud
Love is not noble
Love is not virtuous

Love does not control
Love does not submit
Love does not judge

Love is not compassion
Love is not charity
Love is not altruism

These are all outward expressions
Borne of ego and desire
Love is free of all these constraints

Love is not an emotion

Love is a mountain
Love is a cloud
Love is a fallen tree

Love is silence
Love is darkness
Love is still

Love is action without movement
Love is language without words
Love is passion without desire

Love abandons self
Love forsakes ego
Love is at one with the All-In-All
Love is the All-In-All
And as you are a part of the All-In-All
You are Love

There are no contradictions in the All-In-All
No paradoxes
If I say one thing then another
The two seeming to conflict
It is a koan for you to learn by

Reconciling such contradictions
  releases you from them
Enriching one's understanding of the All-in-All
For none of it actually exists
Reality is a symbolic construct
  of the idea that created it.

This we call life is but a shadow of greater truths
Obscuring them in a veil of reality

A self-imposed enigma
Expression through constraint

To die therefore is no tragedy
It is, rather, a release
Freeing the spirit to witness
A greater truth than has been known

You cannot see the glories of the life beyond this
You cannot know the miracle
　of unshackled expression
You may not go where you will, when you will
Without the limitation of time and space
You will not know the greater bounty
Until you pass the threshold called death

Yet for many
The fear of death
　is the single most profound obstacle to life
That one both expects and refutes an end to living
Creates a dilemma of the psyche
A paradox of being

As all things must change
So too does the phoenix we call spirit
Moving ever on to new adventures

Nothing is lost
But renews itself again and again
In a different vessel
In a different time and space
But always living
Even changing

To fear death is to fear change
To fear change is to fear life
To fear life is to learn nothing

One who does not fear life does not fear death
Wherefore frighten a man with threat of death
When death is of no consequence to him

This does not mean you renounce life
But there is no expectation
And therefore no remorse

No one dies who is not prepared to die
Therefore do not mourn their passing too much
It is their fate and their choice
And they are not truly dead after all
For death is not an end
It is a renewal of life

Yet do not neglect farewells
Though they are not truly dead
Merely removed from this world
And in time you will surely see them again

Give proper ceremony to the parting

For the body is a precious thing
  and can be difficult to abandon
As can the world of experience familiar to the spirit
For the reassurance of those who have
  left this mortal frame
Bid them fond farewell and toast their travels
And remember them to all

This for the comfort not only of the mourned
But for those who mourn
To purge themselves of sorrow

Do it without undue ritual
But in joy and remembrance
To make the parting done

We each live many lives
We live them all at once
We live them in succession
We live them asunder

Each life has its path
Each life plays its part
You are the actor and the writer
The one among many
The many into one

They all exist in the Forever-Now
Speaking with one another
Guiding one another
Choosing one's destiny moment by moment
As if it was ever thus

There is nothing that cannot be altered
If one desires it enough
Be certain of your desires
Mark closely your thoughts
For they create your path
Your fate is manifest
According to your deeds

Know this, and you can change your life at will
Control your destiny
By the choices you make

So do not concern yourself with who you have been
Better to know who you are
For who you are is the culmination of all you have been
It is already within you

And do not dwell on the future
The Forever-Now abides in the moment
Already at your fingertips
The future is the garden we sow
Harvest when it is due
Not before

There is no predestined fate
And there are no accidents
All is set
The future by the past
All is in motion
The future and the past

Fact is fiction given substance
Truth is imagination given form
Everything that is real is also unreal
Everything that is unreal is also real

There is no paradox here
All you perceive is valid and complete
Your dreams are part of that perception
So too your fantasies and visions

They exist not just in your mind
But in the mind of the All-In-All
There is no such thing as no-thing
For once given a name it is given a reality

You are not your self
You are the perception of self
Of action and experience
Of memory and imagination
These things define who you are

But they are not you
You are an aspect of the All-In-All
A shard of creation
A heterogeneous nondividual

Your body is a vibrant sculpture
A vessel of awareness
A vehicle of experience

It is one of many you will have
All designed with but one purpose
To explore and discover the All-In-All
Which is to say – oneself

All of reality is yours to command
And as you change so too reality changes
You are not at the mercy of the elements
You are not powerless against
 an uncompromising world
This world and everything in it
Is created by you
Can be changed by you
And can be destroyed in an instant if you so choose

We are born of the earth
And of the spirit of the earth
And in death are returned to the earth

We are therefore intimately connected with the earth
And with the spirit of its manifestation

What we do unto ourselves
The earth echoes
Disaster, tempest and drought
Famine, plague and blight
All are caused by our collective thoughts and deeds

Thoughts are boomerangs
They will return
Manifest in your reality

Yet it is in disaster that peace abides
Carried on its shoulders like a child
Borne forward by tribulation
This is the way of all things
The process of renewal
Surrender to the child
And to the way of its bearer
Then the change will not be so cruel

For in the great adventure change is inevitable
It is in the very nature of things
You are not the same person you were
  in your last life
Or five years ago
Or yesterday

In time all things are renewed
To be still is to be nothing
With every second you gain experience
That extends your awareness of self

Even as you sleep you grow
Through the moment called Forever-Now
Moving ever forward to a greater you

With every thought you express the All-In-All
With every deed you reflect the All-In-All
This is why you exist
To discover self through expression
There is nothing more worth your regard

Through finite means we grow and learn
Until the means are abandoned

In the understanding of the infinite one is alone

It is unspoken and unseen
It is personal
It cannot be shared
For to do so binds it to reality
To the corporeal
To the senses

It can be expressed only in silence and darkness
Beyond words
Beyond thought
As we each come to our own understanding
Of the All-In-All

In the understanding of the All-In-All
Fear not for your self

You are unique and will always be so
For as you create your nature changes
But your identity will not
We are all unto ourselves
Elemental and entire

And as your body is an expression of your self
What you see in others is also a reflection of self
Likewise –
What you see of the world
  reflects your view of the world
As your view of the world reflects your self
For who you are is defined by your world
And your world is defined by you

If you desire to change the world
Know the change must come from within
Only by changing your self
Can you change the world around you
To affect the hearts and minds of others
Begin with your self

Begin with the thought
Thought into action driven by desire
You interact with this world through the senses
But also through transcendent communion
The physical and the non-physical

These are the paths to understanding
The symbols of life:
Vision, sound, taste and touch
Color, language, food and form
Art, music and myth
Life, death and renewal

You do not have a body
You are your body
You do not have feelings
You are your feelings
You do not have thoughts
You are your thoughts

Your experience of the world
Is as an expression of self
You are the wellspring of existence
The All-In-All

You are not your body
You have a body
You are not your feelings
You have feelings
You are not your thoughts
You have thoughts

You experience the world
As something of it and apart from it
You are the consequence of all things
An expression of the All-In-All

There is no such thing as miracle
That which we call miracle
Is a natural process of the All-In-All

To see a sunrise is a miracle
To watch an ant toil is a miracle
To witness a child grow is a miracle
To hear a bird's call is a miracle
To touch an ancient oak is a miracle
To breath and to live is a miracle

All of life is a miracle
And none of it we truly understand

Since before the beginning
Before eternity
When there was no Time, no Space
In the spark that was and will yet be
Before the One
When there was only itself
When understanding was not yet understood
When consciousness was not yet conscious
When there was naught but the potential
Of unrealized creation

Being without form
Knowing without wisdom
Love without desire
Cause without effect
Origin without end

The observer and observed
The One and the Naught
Vast beyond limit
Without measure

The question and answer
Without reason or choice
Without chaos or order
Forever searching, forever found

Elusive and obvious
Obscure and palpable
Forever changing
Eternally the same
The singularity
The All

From this emerges duality
And existence as we know it
The paradox of life
The All-In-All

It is manifest in every experience
Yet it is not the experience
It is in the smile of a child
Yet it is not the child
It is in the words of a great sage
Yet it cannot be found in words

To know it is to know the Truth
Yet there is no One Truth
It is nothingness
Yet there is not a thing that does not exist within it

It is known to you
Yet you do not know it
It is all that you perceive
Yet you do not perceive it

Such is the nature of the nameless
And having now been named
It is beyond these words

It is unmanifested Truth
Once expressed it is bound by limitation
According to the form one creates
And yet in the act of creation it can be known
As an aspect of the All-In-All

One cannot define the All-In-All
By the symbols of reality
One cannot in limitation
Know it fully and completely
Not as long as it has a name

Reality is, by its very nature, limitation
It is not the whole of existence
But the part in which we choose to live
The part we have created for the great adventure

To focus our efforts
To harness our wills
To learn the nature of our selves

It gives us structure without constancy
Makes us ignorant yet curious
Bestows as it withholds
Compelling us to act, learn and grow

It is the limitations of this world
That give meaning to our lives
It is the little truths discovered
That reveal the greater truth obscured

Truth is mutable and capricious
The fewer truths you entrust
The more secure is your reality
But the less certain is your path
No one truth holds the key to everything
No one key opens every door

When you are so overwhelmed by truths
That nothing is sensible any more
You will be closer to understanding
The All-In-All is not so easily caged

For the truth is:
You cannot know the unknowable
You cannot put faith in the uncertain
And you cannot trust the senses of this world

Only through imagination can one separate
Fact from fallacy
Delusion from desire
And truth from theory

To know nothing is to know everything
To believe in nothing is the only certainty
To trust in nothing is to be open to all

Then as your truth is changed
Your understanding altered
Your vision becomes more clear
And the limitations of this world
Are not so snug

There are many tales that describe
   in myth and metaphor
The dawn of discernment
The beginning of consciousness
The setting apart of infinite selves
From the knowing unknowingness of the All

With this was also born memory
A constraint of mind from the infinite Now
To the arrowed perception of time

And the cleaving of providence
Into fate and free will
Destiny and choice
Two sides to the same coin

Two parts of the same aspect
The polarity of existence

These constraints free us
These distinctions enable us
But they also blind us
They also inhibit us

We are not so free that we can see
All there is to know
We are not so free that we can know
All there is to see

Yet you are a creative being
You make your body move and dance
Invent words and symbols to communicate
Build realities daily in which to explore

You produce works of art
Known and unknown
Conscious and unconscious
In thought, sound, light and form

From the cells of your body
 to the universe you perceive
All of it is your own personal creation
Perfect in every regard
Conceived through consciousness
Made real by desire

The artistry of self is the most profound thing there is
It is expressed in every aspect of your life

That is how powerful you are

And yet
There is no such thing as perfection
All be-ing is in a state of becoming
Not becoming perfect
But becoming more itself

Perfection implies completion
An unsurpassable point of evolvement
Beyond which there can be no further gain

To be perfect is to be still
To be still is to stagnate
Nothing in all of existence is perfect
It is forever changing
Eternally evolving

The only true perfection
Is in that which moves in accord with the All-In-All
Without hindrance or hesitation
In harmony with the changes
That are, after all, an expression of self

To live therefore is impossible without purpose
But to know your purpose
  is not always clear
To know your purpose and fulfill it
  is not always possible
To fulfill your purpose and learn from it
  is not always easy
To learn from life's purpose and be happy
  can be hardest of all
And yet to be happy
  is all the purpose one needs in life
The lessons will be learned
You will be fulfilled
And content

To this end
The most important things to know are
How to live
How to die
How to know self
All else is fleeting and insubstantial

The best education has these goals at its heart
The best education is bespoke to each
The best education is absent dogma or judgment
The best education is free

Avoid setting one point-of-view over another
To do so is to blinker perception

Shed all prejudice
Yet be discriminating in thought
A choice can be changed
A bias cannot

Indeed, the only thing
  that has ever been the cause of war
Is dogma
Religious, political, social and psychological
It has many guises:
Doctrine Creed Faith Philosophy
Policy Principle Opinion Ethics
Facts Statistics Data Truth

All are equally imperfect and corruptible
Including the words set before you now

Believe in nothing absolutely
To do so only binds the mind
Building walls of ignorance and prejudice
For fear of what lies beyond
Abandon all systems of belief
And the walls will tumble

For he who understands his fears understands himself
He who overcomes his fears is subject to no one.

The essence of dogma is not what it teaches
But how it teaches it
It has no power save that which you give it
Allowing others to rule over you

It is to walk in the steps of another

For those who need fences
For those who need guidance
Be content you have not strayed
But know also the choice is yours
To follow or to lead
And in time to see over the fence
Of self-imposed limitation
And go beyond

The only freedom you have
The only freedom you need
Is the freedom to choose

Freedom is not a right to be asserted
It is a state of being
An expression of self

It does not find fault in others
Or bestow the right to judge another
One cannot condemn in the name of freedom

You are responsible only to yourself
Accept your thoughts and actions as a part of you

And allow others this same freedom
For they are a part of your reality
As you are a part of theirs
You are together bound by universal nature
The oneness of all things
The All-In-All

True freedom must be twofold
The freedom to act or be still
The freedom to go or to stay
The freedom to speak or be silent
The freedom to live your own life as you choose

True freedom must be twofold
The freedom to refuse or accept
The freedom to believe or deny
The freedom to love or despise
The freedom to live in the shadow of another

True freedom must be twofold
It cannot be given but must be allowed
It cannot be taken but must not be denied
It cannot be forced but must be chosen
It cannot be known but must be lived
True freedom must be twofold

Freedom is that which allows one
To do as they will
To act as they will
To think as they will
To love or hate as they will
To be as they will

True freedom comes from within
In the full acceptance of self
Requiring no-one's consent
Needing no laws to confer it or enforce it
It is not bequeathed by society
But is an emotional knowingness
Unique to each person

To this end
The ideal society is one that has no government
No hierarchy of leadership
No need of police or courts
Knows no crime or violence
And harbors no contention

The ideal society is not utopia
But nor is it anarchy
It is the expression of its people
Each acting in accord with their inner natures
In accord with the All-In-All

If everyone were this free
There would be like freedom in the society

Unity of purpose
Clarity of goal
Acting from the All-In-All of your being
As a divine expressive individual

This is not only achievable
It is inevitable

Until that day comes
Sound government is needed
Which provides for the physical needs of its citizens
Conferring structure and order
But this alone is insufficient

Sound government should also facilitate
Every citizen's need
For expression, action and learning
According to their desires

A society is defined by those inhabiting it
From the street corner to the nation-state
It is the All-In-All in microcosm

The health of a society is therefore
  reflected in its people

How they work
How they live
Their desires and pleasures
Their hopes and dreams
Their troubles and misfortunes
Their fears and suffering

Look to the lowliest among you
Look to their number
See what your society has become
What you have become
What lesson are you trying to teach your self?

The success of any government can be measured
By how much force it must apply
To maintain itself
The more oppressed its people
The more likely and inevitable
Will be its eventual downfall

Therefore
Those who seek power should not lead
Those who seek fortune should not lead
Those who seek fame and recognition
  should not lead
Those who seek prestige and status should not lead
Only those who have nothing to gain
  and nothing to prove
Are suited to lead

They are invisible, yet open
Strong, yet yielding
Decisive, yet receptive

It matters not how these people come to lead
Whether by consensus or assumption
And it matters not their misdemeanors or private weaknesses
If they act in accord with these values the rule will be fruitful
And serve all to the betterment of their lives

The secret to good government is not to govern
The secret to power is to be powerless
The secret to knowledge lies in ignorance
Only through utter simplicity can one know the infinite

The more laws a society needs
The more limited it is
Where conduct is dictated by social norms
So the moral level of a society can be appraised
Its culture understood
Its people known
And your self revealed

What you see around you reflects who you are
Change the world and you change your self
Change your self and you change the world

Manage society
  as you would manage your own body
Restrain from abjuration or excess
Be purposeful in your thoughts
Nurturing in your deeds
And know that to grow is to change
Not merely expand

Do not hate war
But rather, love peace
Do not condemn injustice
But rather, laud integrity
And do not disdain another
Rather praise that which is noble in them

To oppose is to contend
And in so doing you only reinforce
That you would subdue
You cannot defeat a man who refuses to fight
For in his compliance you are yourself defeated

One must be free to change
And one must change to grow
For without growth there can be no death
And without death there can be no renewal
And the great adventure is wasted

Epilogue

These words are inadequate
Language itself a limitation
Insufficient and misleading
For the All-In-All can have no name
Who would set such a limit upon it?

When you no longer need such words
You will be closer to understanding
  what words cannot convey

What one means when you give it a name
Is not what one means
It cannot be defined by a mere word
Or a million books full of words
To name it is to confine it
And understanding becomes impossible

In years to come
When my body is dust
  and the memory of this life is faded
I will return to continue my mission
As do we all

Until then these words are all I have
Do not try to explain to another
  the meaning of these words

They are for you to find your own meaning
Your own understanding
And do not let another use these words
 to gain power over you
They are not chains but beacons

Pursue happiness according to your desires
And permit others the same by right
Follow your path in light and love
According to your will

May joy and prosperity be always your wish
This being so – you will have it
And in parting let me say to all who read these words
They are given freely
With love and good intentions
But if any part of what you read herein
Does not fit well with you
Do not wear it
Abandon it
Find another teacher
It is a coat tailored, after all, to my reality
And mine alone

Seek your own answers
Find your own path
The only reason for be-ing is to experience
And the only reason to experience is to know Self
There can be no greater truth that this
There can be no simpler goal

— ∞ —

In love I leave these words
May they help guide you on your path
Until you no longer need them

— ∞ —

Tobias

www.ingramcontent.com/pod-product-compliance
Lightning Source LLC
Chambersburg PA
CBHW040802150426
42811CB00081B/2358/J